SPORTS FROM COAST TO COAST™

BASEBALL

RULES, TIPS, STRATEGY, AND SAFETY

— JASON PORTERFIELD —

rosen publishing's
**rosen
central**®

New York

Published in 2007 by The Rosen Publishing Group, Inc.
29 East 21st Street, New York, NY 10010

First Edition

Library of Congress Cataloging-in-Publication Data

Porterfield, Jason.
Baseball: rules, tips, strategy, and safety/Jason Porterfield.—1st ed.
    p. cm.—(Sports from coast to coast)
Includes bibliographical references and index.
ISBN-13: 978-1-4042-0991-6
ISBN-10: 1-4042-0991-3 (lib. bdg.)
1. Baseball—Juvenile literature. I. Title. II. Series.

GV867.5.P67 2007
796.357—dc22

                                                                2006012921

Manufactured in the United States of America

CONTENTS

CHAPTER ONE

Baseball's History

Town ball was an early version of baseball. In town ball, the batter (*above*) was called a "striker," a term still in baseball's official rules.

Baseball is among the oldest and most popular team sports played in the United States. Since its early development in the late 1830s, the sport has undergone many changes. Yet it still remains connected to its earliest traditions. Baseball has evolved from children's recreation to a spectator sport appreciated by millions. Today, baseball's broad appeal has brought the game to people around the world, particularly in Canada, Japan, and Latin America.

Baseball's Origins

America's national pastime is not a completely original concept. The ancient Greeks, Persians, and Egyptians all played stick-and-ball games, recreationally and for ceremonial purposes. These games were not much like modern baseball, apart from the focus on hitting a ball with a stick. By the Middle Ages, variations of these games had spread to Europe.

Baseball likely originated in one such game, called rounders, brought to North America by English settlers during the 1700s. In rounders, a player hit a ball that had been pitched to him and then tried to run around bases without being called out. There were many local variations on rounders, and nearly as many names for the game, including town ball, one o'cat, four o'cat, goal ball, and baste ball.

Until the 1800s, rounders and all of its forms were considered children's games. For adults, only gentlemen with leisure time played such games, usually at gentlemen's clubs. However, as the 1800s progressed, rounders and its variations became increasingly popular with adults. Teams regularly formed at colleges, at military forts and bases, and anywhere else men found themselves with time for recreation. Towns and villages sometimes formed teams for special events. Problems arose, however, when teams from different places played against each other. Rounders had no set rules, so different teams often played according to different conventions.

Abner Doubleday and Alexander Cartwright

According to legend, baseball was invented in Cooperstown, New York, in 1839. A popular story tells of how a young soldier named Abner Doubleday laid out a baseball diamond in a cow pasture, writing down rules and the proper dimensions of the field. Doubleday later denied the story, and the true origins of the baseball diamond remain a mystery.

Abner Doubleday (*above*) was a major general in the American Civil War and a successful businessman. Historians now doubt that Doubleday had anything to do with the invention of baseball.

We are sure, however, that the first book of baseball rules was published in 1845 by Alexander Cartwright. Called *The Knickerbocker Rules*, it formed the basis for the rules of modern baseball. Cartwright's rules were widely adopted, and by 1866, baseball teams had formed from Oregon to Maine.

At first, baseball was strictly an amateur sport. However, teams soon began paying their better players. In 1869, the Cincinnati Red Stockings became the first wholly professional baseball team. An organization of professional teams called the National League formed in 1876, becoming the first true major league. Other leagues formed to compete with the National League, but most failed within a few years. It wasn't until the formation of the American League, in 1901, that the National League had a worthy rival. In 1903, the best team in each league, the Pittsburgh Pirates of the National League and the Boston Americans of the American League, played against each other in the first World Series. It was a best-of-nine series that Boston won, five games to three.

Baseball Evolves

During the 1880s and 1890s, baseball was a high-scoring game. Around the turn of the century, however, pitchers became more dominant, and scores

This illustration shows a game between the Boston Red Stockings and the Philadelphia Athletics in England in 1874. The two teams played a series to promote baseball in Great Britain, with little success.

dropped. Pitchers at this time had an advantage because the same baseballs were used throughout a game, so the balls became softer and more difficult to hit hard. Instead of relying on power hitting, the offense concentrated on speed and strategy. Teams came to rely more on bunts, stolen bases, and plays like the hit-and-run to score runs.

But a couple of rule changes altered the game again. First, beginning in 1920, the leagues enacted stricter penalties on pitchers who cut or scuffed the ball. Then, a new rule required umpires to change baseballs throughout

Babe Ruth

George Herman "Babe" Ruth (1895–1948) started his career as a successful pitcher for the Boston Red Sox. At the suggestion of a teammate, Ruth was moved to the outfield and given a chance to be an everyday player. In 1919, he set a new single-season record by hitting twenty-nine home runs. The Red Sox sold his contract to the New York Yankees at the end of the season, and Ruth went on to become one of the greatest home-run hitters of all time. He broke his own record by hitting fifty-four home runs in 1920. Ruth's exploits on the field brought in many new fans to baseball. Hitters imitated his big swing, making home runs more common. During his career in New York, Ruth played in seven World Series championships and helped the team win four. He retired in 1935 with 714 career home runs, a record that remained unbroken until Hank Aaron surpassed it in 1974.

Babe Ruth was one of baseball's greatest players for twenty-two seasons, most of them spent with the New York Yankees.

the course of a game. Under these rules, pitchers no longer dominated. With a greater emphasis on power hitting and driving in runs, home-run hitters like Babe Ruth became the new stars.

The Negro Leagues

Until the late 1940s, major league baseball did not allow African American players. However, teams made up exclusively of African Americans were

From 1922 to 1946, center fielder James "Cool Papa" Bell (shown here sliding into third base) was known as the fastest player in the Negro leagues.

common. The first all-black professional team, the Cuban Giants from New York, played their first season in 1885. Eventually, all-black teams joined their own organizations, known collectively as the Negro leagues.

The best known of the Negro leagues were the Negro National League, founded in 1920, and the Eastern Colored League, formed in 1923. The two leagues had folded by the early 1930s but were soon replaced by a reorganized Negro National League (1933) and the Negro American League (1937).

Between 1938 and 1947, the best teams from the Negro National League and the Negro American League played in their own annual World Series, similar to the all-white leagues. Many outstanding players competed in the Negro leagues, whose stars included pitcher Satchel Paige, catcher Josh Gibson, and the speedy outfielder James "Cool Papa" Bell.

Integration

Segregation continued until 1945, when the Brooklyn Dodgers' general manager Branch Rickey offered a contract to a Negro league player named Jackie Robinson. When the 1947 season began, many fans and other players were outraged to see a black man playing for a major league team. Robinson took a great deal of abuse both on and off the field, but he maintained his focus and dignity throughout the season. Rickey and especially the Dodgers' shortstop, Pee Wee Reese, continually voiced their support for Robinson, who quietly won over the fans with his grace and his skill.

When the season ended, the Dodgers had won the National League pennant, and Jackie Robinson was voted the major league Rookie of the Year. Robinson played for the Dodgers until he retired in 1956, winning the National League's Most Valuable Player award in 1949 and helping his team win the 1955 World Series.

Other managers, impressed by Robinson's success, began signing African American players. In 1948, Larry Doby of the Cleveland Indians became the first African American to play in the American League. Three other teams were integrated by 1950, and one year after the Negro leagues collapsed, in 1958, all sixteen major league teams had at least one African American player.

This photo shows Jackie Robinson batting in 1947, his first season in the major leagues. Robinson was a very good hitter and an even better base runner.

Baseball Today

Today, the game is played very much like it was in the 1920s, although the face of major league baseball has changed significantly. Hispanic players from Mexico, South America, and the Caribbean began appearing on major league rosters in the 1960s. And at the beginning of the twenty-first century, players from east Asian countries such as Japan and South Korea are having an impact on the major leagues. For example, Japanese-born Ichiro Suzuki, an outfielder for the Seattle Mariners, is particularly popular today.

The St. Louis Cardinals' Albert Pujols (shown here batting) was born outside the United States, in the Dominican Republic. He is emerging as one of the best hitters of the twenty-first century.

There are now roughly 900 major league baseball players, spread among twenty-eight teams across the United States and one—the Toronto Blue Jays—in Canada. In addition, thousands of minor league, college, and high school players compete against each other annually. Around the world, thousands of Little League teams play every summer.

As of 2007, no major league team had signed a woman to a contract, but that may change in the coming years. More girls are playing Little League than ever before, and some are choosing to play baseball in high school instead of softball, the traditional girls' alternative. The amateur-level American Women's Baseball Federation was formed in 1992 to coordinate women's baseball tournaments and promote the sport among women and girls. The organization put together four Women's World Series events from 2001 to 2004, with national teams from the United States, Japan, Canada, and other countries competing.

CHAPTER TWO

The Baseball Field and Player Positions

A pitcher looks in for a signal from his catcher during a game in the 2005 College World Series.

The baseball field consists of two areas: the infield and the outfield. Most of the action during a game takes place in the infield, a diamond-shaped area with a base at each corner. The infield boundaries are formed by the base paths for first and third base and the grass line marking the beginning of the outfield.

Home plate, the bottom point of the baseball diamond, is the main focus of play during a game. On either side of home plate are the batter's boxes, six-foot-by-three-foot (1.8 meters by 0.9 meters) rectangles painted in the dirt, where the batter stands and waits for the pitch. A fence called a backstop prevents any loose balls or wild pitches from leaving the field behind home plate. At the top of a raised mound in the middle of the infield is the pitching rubber, from which the pitcher throws the ball.

The rubber is officially located 60.5 feet (18.4 m) from home plate. Major league rules state that the top of the pitching rubber may be no more than ten inches (25.4 centimeters) higher than home plate.

Going counterclockwise from home plate is first base, succeeded by second and third. From third base, a base runner returns to home plate. The base paths are all the same length, 90 feet (27.4 m) from one base to the next. First, second, and third bases are all slightly raised square cushions, while home plate is a five-sided rubber slab set into the ground.

Players waiting to bat or take the field sit on benches placed inside an area called a dugout. Dugouts may be as simple as a roofless enclosure made up of chain-link fencing, or they may be solidly built structures of cinderblocks and concrete. Traditionally, the home team takes the dugout along the first-base side. Fields also have special areas called bullpens, where pitchers warm up before entering a game.

The Pitcher and Catcher

All of the action in a baseball game begins with the pitcher, who throws the ball toward home plate for batters to try to hit. Pitchers also make plays on balls hit near the mound and try to keep base runners from advancing. There are two

Catchers, like the one shown here, require more protective equipment than players at other positions.

15

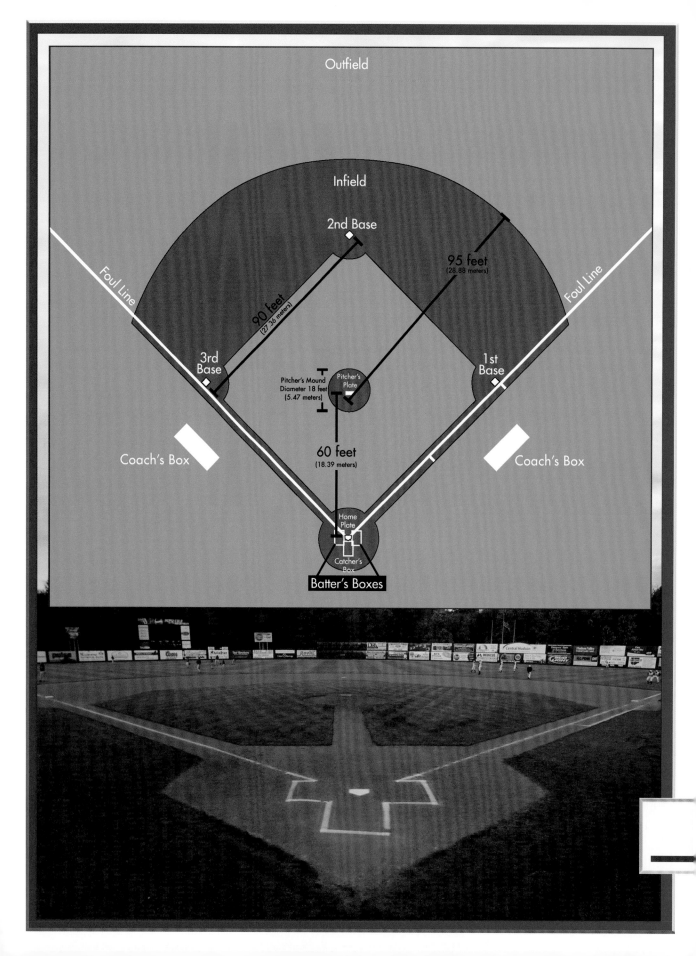

types of pitchers: starters and relievers. When the starter gets tired or pitches poorly, a relief pitcher comes in. In youth leagues, the starter often pitches the whole game. However, in major league baseball, the starter usually lasts for six or seven innings. After that, a middle reliever pitches for an inning or two. Then, another reliever—the closer—pitches the last inning or two to finish the game.

On defense, catchers have the most demanding job on the field. They crouch behind the plate on every pitch, catching the ball and returning it to the pitcher. They also "call" the game, using hand signals to indicate to the pitcher which pitch to throw and where. In addition, catchers try to throw out runners stealing bases and tag out runners trying to score.

The catcher is the most heavily armored player on the field, wearing a helmet, a face mask with throat guard, an athletic cup, shin guards, a bulky glove with extra padding, and a chest protector. All of this gear protects the catcher from errant pitches and foul tips, and also during the occasional collision with a base runner trying to make it to home plate.

On Defense: Playing the Field

Players on defense are either infielders or outfielders. Individual positions come with their own special responsibilities, and the better teams work together seamlessly and play good team defense.

Each of the bases is defended by a fielder. The first baseman guards the area around first base. The second baseman covers second base and most of the territory between first and second. The third baseman covers the area around third. The shortstop takes up position between second base and third base and fields the entire surrounding area. Because they

This diagram *(facing page, top)* shows the placement of the bases and the pitcher's mound, along with the outfield. At bottom, a typical baseball field sits ready for action.

This outfielder is making a strong throw from the outfield.

must cover so much territory, shortstops are usually the quickest and most nimble players on a team. Typically, shortstops and second basemen are more agile than the first and third basemen, since they must cover areas both to their right and left and make throws from difficult angles.

The outfield is covered by the left fielder, the center fielder, and the right fielder. The outfield technically includes all of the area beyond the base paths, although infielders usually make plays on balls hit between the base paths and the outfield grass line. Any grounders, line drives, or fly balls hit beyond the infield become the responsibility of the outfielders.

Outfielders must be fast and coordinated. A strong, accurate throwing arm is also a desired trait. Of the three outfielders, the center fielder has the most territory to cover, and so this player is usually the fastest and most athletic.

Foul lines extending from home plate along the base paths to first and third and beyond mark the side boundaries of the field. The area outside this line is called foul territory. Usually, the farthest boundary of the outfield is marked by a curved wall or fence. Fly balls landing beyond this boundary are home runs. Many fields have foul poles where the foul line meets the wall or fence. These rise high above the field and serve as extensions of the foul lines, helping umpires judge whether a fly ball hit into the stands is fair or foul.

No-Hitters

One of the most impressive pitching feats is throwing a no-hitter. This is a game in which the opposing team fails to get a single hit. For most pitchers, throwing a no-hitter is a once-in-a-lifetime event, though some major league players accomplished the feat multiple times. Hall of Famer Nolan Ryan holds the record, having pitched seven no-hitters. A pitcher may allow walks during a no-hitter, and the team that fails to get a hit may even score runs. In 1964, for example, Ken Johnson of the Houston Astros pitched a no-hitter against the Cincinnati Reds and still lost the game after a run scored on an error!

Nolan Ryan, shown here playing in 1986 for the Houston Astros, pitched in the major leagues for a record twenty-seven years.

Perfect games are even rarer feats. They are no-hitters in which the pitcher retires all twenty-seven batters in a row. Since 1903, there have been only fifteen perfect games pitched in the major leagues. The last occurred in 2004, when Randy Johnson of the Arizona Diamondbacks pitched a perfect game against the Atlanta Braves.

On Offense: The Batting Order

Everyone playing in the field gets a chance to bat. The exception to this rule is the American League, in which pitchers can be replaced in the lineup by designated hitters, who bat but do not play the field. Managers cannot change the batting order in the middle of the game, so the best hitters usually bat in the first few spots in the lineup. This way, they have more chances to get on base.

A batter strides into a pitch. To generate power, batters shift their weight from their back foot to their front foot and turn their hips as they swing.

The first spot in the batting order, the leadoff position, usually goes to the fastest and most alert base runner. The second and third positions generally go to good hitters who also are speedy on the base paths. The fourth, or cleanup, batter is usually the most powerful hitter on the team, with a proven ability to drive in runs. The bottom slots in the order are usually reserved for the weaker hitters on the team.

A replacement batter, called a pinch hitter, may be inserted into the lineup. However, the original player must then be removed from the game.

Players listen to their coach as he gives instructions before a game. Coaches help players improve in all aspects of play, from hitting and baserunning to fielding and throwing.

Managers and Coaches

Baseball managers are responsible for planning a team's strategy, drawing up the lineup card, and making substitutions during a game. In professional baseball, the manager is assisted by a team of specialized coaches, who focus on fielding, batting, and pitching. Little League and youth league managers usually act as both pitching and hitting coaches, although volunteers or former players may help out.

During the game, the hitting team is aided by base coaches at first base and third base. These coaches watch the action on the field and direct the runners, telling them whether to hold up at the base or advance to the next one. In youth league games, other players often act as base coaches.

Uniforms and Protective Gear

All players and coaches on a team wear identical uniforms, usually made up of cotton pants, a jersey, and a cap. On their feet, players wear cleats, shoes with hard nubs or spikes on the soles designed to give them traction on the dirt base paths. Outfielders sometimes have to look up to field fly balls, so they'll usually wear sunglasses during day games. Batters may wear batting gloves to help them keep their grip on the bat and to protect their hands when they slide into bases.

This infielder is dressed in full uniform, from his cap to his cleats. The button-front jersey is a baseball tradition that dates back to the early days of the sport.

Since most of the baseball season is played in the summer, jerseys are generally short-sleeved. Some teams also have long-sleeved jerseys for colder weather. Professional, college, and high school teams have two different uniforms, one for home games and one for away games.

Unlike football or hockey, baseball is not a game that requires a lot of protective gear. When playing the field, most players do not wear any special protection, although male players usually wear a hard plastic athletic cup to protect the groin region. Batters wear helmets to protect themselves from stray pitches, and some batters also wear special pads to protect elbows, forearms, shins, and the top of their front foot.

Baseball Equipment

Most baseball equipment is standardized to meet specific rules. Fielders' gloves are usually made of stiff leather. The dominant feature of a baseball glove is the basket, the flexible material between the thumb and forefinger in which fielders trap most balls when making a play. Players who throw right-handed wear their gloves on their left hand so that their throwing arm is free. The reverse is true for left-handed players.

Baseballs are about nine inches in circumference. The baseball's core is made of cork or rubber wrapped in layers of synthetic string and rubber and covered with stitched rawhide. Game balls are white with red stitching.

In the major leagues, bats cannot be longer than 42 inches (1.07 m). The bat tapers from the barrel to the narrower grip. The barrel must be less than 2.75 inches (6.99 cm) in diameter. In the major leagues, bats are made of wood, traditionally ash or maple. In Little League games, batters are allowed to use bats made of aluminum, which doesn't break like wood. Aluminum bats are lighter, meaning that players swing them faster, generating faster bat speeds and more power. This additional power would give professional batters an unnecessary advantage, so aluminum bats are not allowed in the major leagues. In addition, baseball purists prefer wooden bats, claiming that the "crack!" of a ball hitting a wooden bat is much more satisfying than the "ding!" produced by an aluminum bat.

CHAPTER THREE

Playing the Game

Right-handed hitters—like the one shown here—turn to the left to face the pitcher. Left-handed hitters, in contrast, stand on the other side of home plate and turn to the right.

Baseball games are played over nine periods of play called innings. The team that scores more runs over the course of those nine innings wins the game. Each inning is divided into two halves, the top and the bottom. The visiting team bats in the top of the inning, while the home team bats in the bottom. The team batting is allowed three outs per inning. After three outs, the other team comes to bat.

Offensive Strategy: At Bat

The batter's first goal is to get safely on base, preferably by hitting a pitch. The best hitters have excellent eye-hand coordination and can hit a ball where there is no fielder to catch it. Once the ball is in play, fielders attempt to make plays to prevent the hitting team from scoring runs. A play ends when the runners on the bases have been called safe or out and the ball is returned to the pitcher.

At the start of a play, the batter stands in the batter's box, ready for the pitch. If the pitch is hittable, the batter may swing at it. On the other hand, the batter has the option of "taking," or not swinging at the pitch. If the batter takes a pitch and it passes through the strike zone, the umpire calls the pitch a strike. (The strike zone is an imaginary space directly over home plate and between the batter's knees and armpits.) If the pitch passes outside the strike zone—whether too high, too low, or off the inside or outside of the plate—the umpire calls the pitch a ball. Patient batters will take four balls and advance to first base with a walk. In many situations, a walk is as good as a hit; it helps to tire out the pitcher, too.

If the batter swings at a pitch and misses, it is a strike. It is also a strike if the batter swings and makes contact but the ball lands in foul territory. The batter is allowed three strikes to put the ball in play. If the pitcher throws three strikes past the batter, it is an out—a

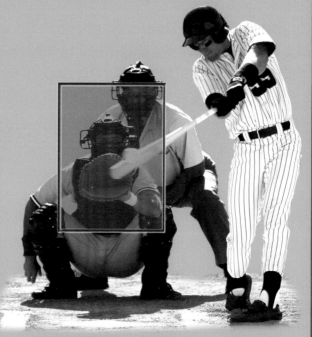

Disciplined hitters wait for the pitcher to throw a pitch in the strike zone.

strikeout. If a batter has two strikes and hits a swinging foul ball, however, he continues to bat.

When a batter makes contact and the ball lands between the foul lines, the ball is considered fair, and the batter must run to first base while fielders attempt to make a play. After hitting the ball, the batter advances to the farthest possible base. A single is a hit on which the batter safely advances to first base; on a double, the batter makes it to second base; on a triple, the batter reaches third. The most desirable hit is a home run, which occurs when a batter makes it all the way back to home to score on his own hit.

Running the Bases

Baserunning is a crucial aspect of the game. The batter becomes a base runner after safely reaching base. In order to score a run, the runner must advance safely to each base and come back to home. Only one runner is allowed on a base at a time, so a runner standing on first must advance to second if the batter puts the ball in play or walks. However, if a runner is on second or third and the previous base is empty, the runner is not forced to advance. If there are less than two out and a ball in the air is caught, a base runner may try to "tag up," or advance to the next base, but only after the catch is made.

Base runners must remain alert and know where the ball is at all times. They seldom stand touching the base during another player's at-bat. Instead, they take a "lead," standing a few feet off base, ready to run if the batter makes contact. Speedy base runners may also try to advance to an open base during a pitcher's windup and delivery. This is called attempting to "steal" a base. Runners planning to steal often take a big lead, making their intentions clear. Instead of winding up and throwing to the plate, an alert pitcher may

Base runners keep a sharp eye on the pitcher as they lead off their base. A runner with quick feet may take three or four steps toward the next base, while slower runners generally stay within a step or two of their base.

try to throw to a base to "pick off" the runner. If a fielder tags the runner off base, the runner is out. If the runner breaks for the next base when the pitcher throws toward home plate, the catcher immediately throws to the base being stolen, where the fielder tries to tag the runner out.

Good technique allows a runner to get around the bases quickly. When running from home to first on an infield ground ball, a runner should "run through" first base, since he can't be tagged out in that situation. If a batter

Base runners should keep to the inside of the base paths as they run. This reduces the time it takes to get around the bases.

hits a ball through the infield, he should immediately be thinking of trying for a double. If the outfielder bobbles the ball, he will have a better chance of making it to second base. Between bases, the runner should travel in as straight a line as possible, listening to a coach's instructions or stopping at the next base and locating the ball quickly. When approaching a base, runners looking to advance further should begin their turn as they approach the base. Then they round the base, stepping on an inside corner as they pass.

If the situation calls for the runner to run hard into a base, sliding is a good way to avoid getting tagged out. The safest slides are made feet-first. Runners should avoid putting a hand down when sliding, as this may cause hand and wrist injuries.

Offensive Strategy: The Sacrifice Bunt

In baseball, a single run can make the difference between winning and losing. For this reason, a manager may call for a batter to sacrifice bunt. For this play, a hitter surrenders his chance to get on base in the interest of moving a teammate forward to second or third base. To execute a sacrifice bunt, the batter holds the bat directly across home plate with one hand on the handle and the other further down the barrel. Instead of swinging hard at the pitch, the batter tries to make soft contact, hitting the ball on the

This batter is using good bunting technique. He holds the bat level with the ground and lets the ball hit the bat, rather than stabbing at it.

ground a few feet away from the plate. Since a fielder has to run in from his position, a base runner will usually have time to advance to the next base on a sacrifice bunt. The batter, however, is usually thrown out at first base.

Defensive Strategy: Pitching

At the heart of a baseball game is the battle between the pitcher and the batter. A successful pitcher uses a combination of different pitches and pitch locations to either strike the batter out or force him to hit balls he would prefer not to hit.

There are many different pitches used in baseball. The ball will act differently depending on how the pitcher grips the ball, the motion of the wrist as it is released, and the speed at which it is thrown. Common pitches include the fastball, the changeup, the curveball, the split-finger, and the knuckleball.

To generate as much power as possible, pitchers rock back and wind up for the pitch. Although arm strength is important for a pitcher, it is through lower body strength that a pitcher creates momentum to throw fastballs. A high kick and a good push off the pitching rubber allow a hard-throwing pitcher to avoid strains and injuries to his elbow and shoulder. Durable pitchers also follow through properly after releasing the pitch, bending forward to the opposite side of the body from the throwing arm, ending with the armpit just over the knee.

Defensive Strategy: Fielding

As the batting team tries to bring runners around to score, the fielders try to get them out before they can accomplish their goal. There are several ways in

This pitcher winds up before delivering to home plate. Pitchers grip the ball differently to produce different results. For example, pitchers use a four-seam grip (*inset*) to throw a straight fastball.

which fielders make outs. If the ball is hit in the air, they can catch it for an out. If the ball is hit on the ground, they can catch the ball and tag the runner with it, or they can step on a base ahead of the runner while in possession of the ball. This last play, called a force out, applies if there is another runner on the base directly behind the one the runner is on, forcing him to advance.

If a fielder has the ball in hand and cannot tag the runner himself, he must throw the ball to the infielder most likely to make an out. When infielders get

Like this shortstop, infielders should position their whole bodies in front of ground balls, which can bounce unpredictably as they hit the infield dirt.

Baseball Statistics

Some say the real history of baseball is told in numerical records called statistics. They allow fans to compare players from different eras.

For pitchers, the important statistics are traditionally the earned run average (ERA), games won, and strikeouts recorded. ERA represents the average number of earned runs allowed by a pitcher per nine innings pitched. In 1968, St. Louis Cardinal pitcher Bob Gibson recorded the lowest ERA in major league history for a pitcher throwing at least 300 innings. That year, his ERA was an amazing 1.12.

Nolan Ryan holds the modern record for most strikeouts in a season by a pitcher. He struck out 383 batters in 1973.

Today, a twenty-win season is a major pitching achievement. In the early 1900s, Walter Johnson and Cy Young both won more than thirty games in consecutive seasons!

Hitters have their own statistics, too. The most telling hitting statistic is a player's batting average. This number indicates the proportion of times a batter gets a hit to reach base safely. A batting average of .300 is considered pretty good in the major leagues. The highest average ever by a major-league player in a single season was .424. Rogers Hornsby recorded this average in 1924, playing for the St. Louis Cardinals. No batter has hit better than .400 since Ted Williams hit .406 in 1941. The highest career average in major league history is .367, established by Ty Cobb in a career spanning from 1905 to 1928.

two runners out on the same play, it is called a double play. Double plays are rather common. For the rare triple play, the fielders get three runners out on the same play.

If a fielder drops a ball or throws wildly and the runner is safe, it is called an error. To avoid errors, a fielder uses good technique. To catch a fly ball or pop-up, he runs quickly to get under the ball and secures it in the glove using his bare hand. With ground balls, fielders should kneel or get close to the ground directly in front of the ball. They should keep their eyes on the ball all the way, until it rolls or hops into the glove.

Umpires

Baseball's rules seldom change. When they do, the changes are added to the official rule book, a document studied by all umpires, managers, and

Plays at home plate are often close and confusing. Here, a runner is called "safe" by the home plate umpire after sliding to beat the tag.

coaches. On the field, the umpires (umps) enforce the rules. In the pros, there are at least three umps on the field for regular games, and usually four. The ump behind home plate wears a face mask, chest protector, and shin guards in case of foul balls or wild pitches. The other umps take up positions near the bases. In Little League and youth league games, there are usually only two umpires, one behind the plate and one in the field.

Umpires make the call on whether a pitch is a ball or a strike, whether a ball lands fair or foul, and whether a runner is safe or out. They have the right to check bats and balls for illegal modifications. Umpires may also eject players and managers from a game for arguing or breaking the rules. If an umpire does a good job, the game runs smoothly. For this reason, there's an old baseball saying: "The best umpires are the ones you never notice."

CHAPTER FOUR

Getting Involved

Baseball is a team game that requires contributions from players with different skills. The best pitchers are rarely the best hitters, the fastest runners are not necessarily the best fielders, and the most powerful sluggers may strike out more than anyone else on the team. Every team has room for a player who is willing to work to improve. Like most team athletes, baseball players must work hard to keep in shape, improve their knowledge of the game, and maintain their form. Regular practice, exercise, and observing other players can help a player advance his or her skills.

In practice, teams do drills that simulate situations likely to occur during a real game. Here, a base runner practices sliding under an infielder's tag.

Stretching and Warm-Up

Playing baseball requires coordination, flexibility, speed, and strength. Before games and practice, players usually spend twenty minutes to an hour stretching their muscles and warming up to avoid injuries. Commonly, pregame warm-up exercises are light, usually a jog around the field before stretching. It is important to be in good physical condition for a wide range of activities before joining a team. Many players run and do weight training to get into shape before the season begins.

Drills and Fundamental Skills

Often, the focus at practice is on drills. For these, team members practice the same activity over and over again until the motions become second nature. Pitchers work with catchers on their control, concentrating on placing the ball over particular parts of home plate. They may also try new pitches in practice, or they may experiment with changing the way they throw a certain pitch to get better results.

For their part, outfielders "shag" fly balls and work on making strong, accurate

Regular stretching helps players increase their range in the field and their ability to make difficult plays.

37

Baseball and Steroids

Weight training is a good way for professional ballplayers to stay in shape for the long season. However, most physicians recommend that young athletes do not start serious weight training until they are at least fifteen or sixteen years old. Rapidly growing bodies of younger athletes are much more likely to suffer torn ligaments and muscles from weight lifting.

Recently, the issues of steroids and other performance-enhancing drugs have received a lot of attention in the media. Cheaters can use steroids to become stronger and faster. However, studies have related steroid use to severe health problems, including premature heart attacks, strokes, liver tumors, kidney failure, and serious psychiatric problems. It goes without saying that players at all levels should avoid steroids.

Not only are there physical dangers to using steroids, but you may also lose the privilege of playing on a team. Minor league teams have very strict policies forbidding drug use, as do many high school and college programs. In most cases, the steroid user is suspended from the team for several games after the first offense and banned after the second. Although evidence indicates that steroid use has been a problem in major league baseball as far back as the early 1990s, MLB began testing for steroids only in 2003.

Both Barry Bonds (*top*) and Mark McGwire (*bottom*) have been accused of artificially enhancing their skills with steroids.

throws to the appropriate base. Infielders scoop up grounder after grounder and work on their footwork and throwing form. They also work on catching infield pop-ups, calling "Mine!" or "I got it!" to let their teammates know to stay out of the way.

Batters work on their swing, and they practice hitting pitches that give them trouble. They also work on bunting technique. Base runners may practice running technique, getting a good lead, stealing bases, and sliding to avoid tags.

Practice may also include other running drills and weight training. For all athletes, strong core muscles (abdominal and back muscles) are important to performing well. For hitters, strong wrists and forearms are the key to bat control. You can ask your coach for specific exercises to develop these muscles.

The Season

The length of a baseball season depends on the league. For Little Leaguers and other youth league players, practices begin in mid- to late spring, with the season played out over the summer months. Teams typically play one or two games per week.

Youth league championships are usually awarded to the team with the best record, though sometimes the top teams compete in a playoff game. In high school and college baseball, the best two teams in a district or athletic conference compete in a championship game, with the winner taking home the district trophy. The winning team may move on to regional competition and even advance as far as a state or national championship game.

Major league teams play 162 games, with the season beginning in April and ending in late September or early October. The first round of the playoffs begin soon after, with the winners advancing to the league championship series, a seven-game playoff. The league champions advance to the World Series, which starts around the last week of October. The winner of the best-of-seven World Series is declared world champion.

The ultimate prize in baseball is winning the World Series. Here, the Boston Red Sox celebrate their World Series victory in 2004. Prior to that, the Red Sox had not won a World Series since 1918.

Joining the Game

If you would like to play in the World Series someday, you have to start playing. Getting involved in baseball is easy, as many towns have leagues for all age groups. Signing up for Little League is usually as simple as showing up for the first practice. In some larger communities with many teams, there may be tryouts and a player draft, in which managers from each team select new players, one by one. Many locales also have leagues for players too old for Little League. Inquire at your local community center if you would like to play. Players interested in joining a middle school or junior high team often try out to earn a place on the team. Those looking to improve their skills in the off-season may attend baseball camps, often run by former professional players. Older players usually have to try out for high school or college teams. Adults may play in town or neighborhood leagues.

Community or municipal leagues, often sponsored by local businesses, are generally open to anyone within the age requirement. The teams usually provide uniforms, balls, helmets, and often bats. Players typically bring their own gloves and cleats.

Even if there are no formal leagues nearby, you can always form

Though baseball is traditionally considered a boys' sport, the game is becoming more popular among girls, especially at the middle school and high school levels.

a team of your own with friends and neighbors, improvising your own rules to fit your situation. Many such games are played in backyards and parks every day, often with just a handful of people, a ball, and a bat. Even if you prefer to watch instead of play, spending a summer day at a baseball game can be a great experience, connecting you to a long tradition.

GLOSSARY

batting average A personal statistic indicating the percentage of times a
batter gets a hit. Batting average is arrived at by dividing the number
of hits by the number of at bats.

bunt To hit a baseball lightly, without swinging the bat.

draft A selection process in which teams take turns claiming players from
a common pool.

earned run average (ERA) A personal statistic for pitchers. It indicates the
average number of earned runs a pitcher allows per nine innings.

fly ball A ball batted into the air.

grounder A batted ball that rolls or bounces along the ground.

inning In a baseball game, a period of play during which each team gets a
turn to bat; a full baseball game lasts nine innings.

integrate To make open to people of all racial and ethnic groups.

lineup A list of batters arranged according to the order in which they
will bat.

pitcher The member of a baseball team who throws the ball for a batter to
try to hit.

segregate To separate based on race or ethnicity.

shag In baseball, to practice catching fly balls in the outfield.

statistics Numbers and data used to evaluate the performance of baseball players.

steroids Hormones that can be used topically, ingested, or injected to promote muscle growth.

synthetic Produced artificially.

umpire An official at a baseball game who oversees play.

windup The beginning of a pitcher's motion, prior to delivering the pitch.

FOR MORE INFORMATION

Little League International
539 US Route 15 Hwy.
P.O. Box 3485
Williamsport, PA 17701
(570) 326-1921
Web site: http://www.littleleague.org

Major League Baseball
The Office of the Commissioner of Baseball
245 Park Avenue, 31st Floor
New York, NY 10167
(212) 931-7800
Web site: http://www.mlb.com

National Baseball Hall of Fame
25 Main Street
Cooperstown, NY 13326
(888) 425-5633
Web site: http://www.baseballhalloffame.org

Web Sites

Due to the changing nature of Internet links, Rosen Publishing has developed an online list of Web sites related to the subject of this book. This site is updated regularly. Please use this link to access the list:

http://www.rosenlinks.com/scc/base

FOR FURTHER READING

Forker, Dom, et al. *Baffling Baseball Trivia*. Madison, WI: Main Street Press, 2004.

Gutman, Dan. *Baseball's Greatest Games*. New York, NY: Penguin Books USA Inc., 1994.

Kreutzer, Peter, and Ted Kerley. *Little League's Official How-to-Play Baseball Book*. New York, NY: MasterVision Inc., 1990.

Light, Jonathan Fraser. *The Cultural Encyclopedia of Baseball*. Jefferson, NC: McFarland & Company, Inc., 2005.

McKissack, Patricia, and Fredrick McKissack. *Black Diamond: The Story of the Negro Baseball Leagues*. New York, NY: Scholastic Paperbacks, 1998.

Ripken, Cal, et al. *Play Baseball the Ripken Way: The Complete Illustrated Guide to the Fundamentals*. New York, NY: Random House, 2004.

Ritter, Laurence S. *The Story of Baseball*. 3rd ed. New York, NY: William Morrow and Company, 1999.

Stewart, Mark. *Baseball: A History of the National Pastime*. New York, NY: Franklin Watts, 1998.

Thorn, John, ed., et al. *Total Baseball, Completely Revised and Updated: The Ultimate Baseball Encyclopedia*. Wilmington, DE: SportClassic Books, 2004.

BIBLIOGRAPHY

Alexander, Charles. *Our Game: An American Baseball History*. New York, NY: Henry Holt and Company, 1991.

Frommer, Harvey. *Primitive Baseball: The First Quarter-Century of the National Pastime*. New York, NY: Atheneum, 1988.

Koppett, Leonard. *Koppett's Concise History of Major League Baseball*. New York, NY: Carroll and Graf Publishers, 2004.

Nemec, David. *The Rules of Baseball: An Anecdotal Look at the Rules of Baseball and How They Came to Be*. New York, NY: Lyons & Burford, 1994.

Okrent, Daniel. *Nine Innings*. New York, NY: Ticknor & Fields, 1985.

Seymour, Harold. *Baseball: The People's Game*. New York, NY: Oxford University Press, 1990.

INDEX

About the Author

Jason Porterfield is a writer and a researcher living in Chicago. He has written more than a dozen books for Rosen Publishing, on topics ranging from American history to the human impact on the environment. While growing up in Virginia, Porterfield was an outfielder for his hometown Little League team, the Newport Cubs. He bats and throws left-handed. His cousin, the late Bob Porterfield, pitched in the major leagues from 1948 to 1959. In 1953, Bob led the American League in wins (22) and shutouts (9) as a pitcher for the Washington Senators.

Photo Credits

Cover (left, top, and field), pp. 1, 15, 16 (bottom), 18, 20, 21, 22, 24, 25, 27, 28, 31 (inset), 36 by Darryl Bautista © The Rosen Publishing Group and Darryl Bautista; cover (right) © ShutterStock; p. 3 © www.istockphoto. com/Charles Silvey; pp. 4, 6, 7, 9, 11 National Baseball Hall of Fame; pp. 8, 12, 14, 19, 29, 31, 38 (bottom) © Getty Images; p. 32 © Icon/SMI; p. 34 © Jim Cummins/Corbis; p. 37 © Sean Justice/Getty Images; 38 (top) © AP/ Wide World Photos; p. 40 © Ron Vesely/MLB Photos via Getty Images; p. 41 © Lee Strickland/Getty Images; back cover (soccer ball) © www.istockphoto. com/Pekka Jaakkola; back cover (paintball gear) © www.istockphoto.com/ Jason Maehl; back cover (football helmet) © www.istockphoto.com/Stefan Klein; back cover (football) © www.istockphoto.com/Buz Zoller; back cover (baseball gear) © www.istockphoto.com/Charles Silvey; back cover (basketball) © www.istockphoto.com/Dusty Cline.

Designer: Nelson Sá; **Editor:** Christopher Roberts
Photo Researcher: Marty Levick